Fierce Aria

poems

Maxima Kahn

Finishing Line Press
Georgetown, Kentucky

Fierce Aria

Publisher: Leah Maines

Editor: Christen Kincaid

Cover & book design by Maxima Kahn

Cover photo by Annie Spratt on Unsplash

Author photo by Don Williams

Printed in the USA on acid-free paper.
Order online: www.finishinglinepress.com
also available on amazon.com

Author inquiries and mail orders:
Finishing Line Press
P. O. Box 1626
Georgetown, Kentucky 40324
U. S. A.

Contents

I
Andante cantabile

II
Adagio mesto

III
Allegro grazioso

This book is dedicated to my parents,
Ruth Anna Putnam (1927-2019) and Hilary Putnam (1926-2016).
Your presence is all over this book.

Fierce Aria

I

Andante cantabile

Winter

All night the ravens
        release
                a black crying
as if they held worlds
      we can never touch.

It's the woods
      where the breathing
            moves
where night
      well, you know.

At some point
      you have to come back
            to your own house.
All the spells of the others
      you have to leave them—even the apple
      the old witch gave.

          You're not going to wake up
             to salvation.
          You know that by now.

But inside
      where the cupboards are filled
             with the familiar
where loneliness languishes   in narrow beds
here
      there is something
         you can build with.

There isn't any choice
         about where to start—always the beginning
      small and limited as it seems:

One rose in a cup
the mouse gnawing the cereal
laundry muttering in a basket.

After that I can't say.
The woods are dark,
        here is the gate—
                    and my own amazement
cries me to sleep.

Harbor Song

Listen, I have to trust the wind
that blows through me, nearly
blows me out, the body's ballad
full of suppressed anger and shimmer

Constant song out over the harbor
like the bell of a lighthouse
off again on again
like the light cutting fog

Listen, the music glides unriveted
to any solid thing, pours down
from some heaven or haven, all agate
and azure and mist we can't catch

The ocean's drenched hymn
swallowing whatever identities
I once clutched, riven now, tide taking
the no longer beautiful, turning it to sand
or brushed bottle glass, color of bruise

Strange ghost, it transforms
as it makes its transit—I'm afraid
of its sway and tidal power
its unhinged and unhinging movement

I'm afraid of the melody
moving like dark water
through my bones, annihilating while
restoring me whole

Yet I am washed or I am nothing—
life is furious song
or it is emptiness—this wrenching
grace, fierce aria is all

Dark Nets

What do you catch in your nets this morning?
Black solitudes, weights of iron and lead.

What do you haul in, what stains the shore?
Veins of tears, hands wringing out the dead,
sleepless eyes, and the mirages of fish
that slip through your dreams at night.

What has whispered by your bedside through the long hours
of your fitful sleep? *Failure, failure, failure.*
The shirt you thought you'd shucked you find clinging to your skin,
wet and wretched and heavy. You can't peel it off.
It becomes you. Dark nets cast over a darker sea.

Lash of water, lash of light.
You lean, looking for something to count on, to number,
and further on, to love,
like walking out to the water's edge, crazy with light.

The Language of Clouds

Sky writes large with a brilliant hand,
    wave and anvil, impending horizon,
clouds stack up like plates,
    white china waiting to fall,
the gods' pellucid writing
    in the advancing squall.

While down on earth we stumble in the fog,
    our gestures hardly able to articulate such light,
wan palettes thinning over greyed canvas,
    thread-bare desire, tired old wants,
our words a muttered air, trailing off before the ends,
    mute icons toward something we don't understand.

Captured ice hangs in the atmosphere, striking us dumb,
    cirrus streaks across the sky, nimbus laden with rain,
cumulus paving cloud streets
               the angels might ride down.

We have no vocabulary to compare with these
    dialects of illumination.
Black waves swallow mountains whole,
    re-write the known
in vast billows
    on which we read signs.

If I could appropriate the language of clouds,
    tune its cold mastery to my mouth,
draw my images in inverted air with noctilucent lines,
    spread myself across the sky in manic hues,
peach-blossom, gun-metal, mauve and turquoise—
    and always be erasing
like the Tibetan sand-masters building grain by grain
    elaborate mandalas to be emptied in the river's flow,

If I could speak in stacked plumes, mock suns
    and errant holes in the sky,
if these distortions were my speech,
    the scud and pileus,
who would I be?
    How does my language write me?

Penumbra

1 a space of partial illumination (as in an eclipse) between the
perfect shadow on all sides and the full light

2 a surrounding or adjoining region in which something exists
in a lesser degree: fringe

maybe we had been talking about this a long time,
the sky growing grey and still, the windows turning to glazed stares

maybe we sat at the wooden table by the window a long time,
the river freezing over inch by inch, snow piling on its banks

maybe the line is just one unit of measurement and not the absolute
as a painter and a poet we might never know

maybe the stone bridge is a metaphor of crossing
maybe it stands for holding hands

maybe the edges of our vision are a habitable country
and the natives are friendlier than we suspect

maybe we will make small notations in the margins
and these will become the whole story or song

maybe there are spaces that link the things between
and are more important than the perfect shadow and the full light

maybe the round edges of our bodies signify a borderland
and not a hard boundary, a place of exploration and entry

maybe nothing is definitive
maybe you would hold my hand

Shades

There are so many shades of daylight.
Today sky-blue and earnest. So many distances
to stretch our eager bodies toward.

Today the painters want to talk about the gaps,
about palette and style, which is a kind of meaning,
in the late 20th century.

But look! we have already entered another,
and in the great democracy of the Unknown,
we are leveled and bewildered.

And look, the poets are scattered,
lost among words as among fragrances in a scent shop.
What verses come from a frozen river?

We are searching the treetops for a brittle harmony,
close to the sky's tornado of blue,
flinging the clouds to the outer margins.

Anything could drop
at any moment and change
the whole equation—

that's why we write and paint and sculpt, why we etch
our figures on steel plates and smear, why
the white walls invite and challenge us.

Every day someone goes to work and every night
to sleep—in essence it's all a handshake,
moment's brief touch, our fundamental craving.

Now the icicles are giving way, falling in great lethal crystals to the ground, the snow is being scraped away to uncover the usual paths, we're readying the way.

In another life, I would become your lover and you mine, in another life there would be more time.

Untranslatable

Even the buildings are calm and implacable,
    even the light, constantly changing,
has a smooth, glassy certainty,

the landscape as placid as ever—
    dark pines against a pale sky,
stark outlines of bare oaks and maples,
    and the river moving forward,
ringing her dark bells,
            a jangling harmony
                  over rocks.

Only our hearts and soft bodies get caught
    in this perpetual tumult,
frames reeling past, out of control,
    to the *clack clack clack* at the end of the roll.

How painful it is to be human
    to have taken this form in this life—
always succumbing to the slow undertow,
    nothing certain but change itself,
never able to voice our whole feeling,
    always coming up short
against the comma, the semi-colon,
            abrupt uncertain endings.

We live our lives in fragmentary sentences,
    untranslatable text, resisting description,
            dangling modifiers, uncertain syntax, we search
for the verb that would make us shine,
    the one language we would speak all day
               if we had time.

Our blood covers everything, our scent and sex—
    we'd keep it if we could,
all of it glistening with earth's lush dew,
    fading fast in perennial disrobing.

If only we could spell it back into being
    with one true language we would sing.

Reading Wright Again

for Charles Wright

Listen to the still thought in the dull
        pencil lying on the desk, how it harbors
secret ambitions, envying the fountain pen
        that luxuriates in a velvet box—
or the humbleness of the four-square notepad,
        wanting to be used, to be used up.

I know what you are thinking—
        rhyming in your tongue, huddled
in your solitudes, observant
        of the weather—I know
about fortitude
        and failure.

How we are blessed with ordinary thought,
        supermarkets, junk mail and lousy weather,
wavering between sleet and snow.
        These missives like bottles
            thrown out over an open sea.

Line and curve and ink-blot
        make a conjuring you and I understand,
linger in some page
        of book and musty library
to well up in other mouths, budding
        like new fruit.

But then the punctuation trips us up—
        its hard hand, cruel-edged rules,
so unforgiving, like a bad parent—foolish and small,
        it wants to steady itself
with obstructions,
        and we allow it—

because we need those confines
        to rein our vagrant
imaginations in, or we see a reflection
        of ourselves in those sad
gestures reappearing
        in every sentence.

All so different from the rock and branch,
        different from the snow—
those lives nothing like our own,
        those dreams
not even what we know
        as dreams.

Just look at the drops of water
        in a shining row
on this branch of blossoming dogwood.

Some Angels

some angels are stirring up the daylight
while i am locked in the madness of this world

with pen in hand, the scattered light of the courtyard
finches uttering their narrative, cars hurrying past

everywhere the remembering and forgetting
i take a deep breath

putting space between the particles of hurt
watch the flicker of shadows on brick

hear the fountain's constant plashing
this morning that smells of still semi-distant autumn

trucks roar down the alley
tear the limbs off trees—still the angels sing

the wind lifts the cover of a poetry book
lying on the glass-top garden table

i feel the slow burn of sadness
we shouldn't have to earn

our welcome, be outside the infinite
looking for a sealed door that isn't

i put pen to page
hear the beating of wings

allow the ache and sadness
the frailness of language

my own inadequacy
the wind and the windchime's song

Changing the Scene

because there's this gap—
inevitable—between what we believe—and what we do—
because we set our ideals among the branches—the high branches—
while our feet keep tracing these circles on the ground—
our feet of clay—and we believe
so deeply—but there are circumstances—no?—both beyond
and well within our control— and we would like so much
to be good—and we also want
so very much to be bad—we are obsessed with freedom—
with choice—and this is where the unravelling
begins—in that sway
between reality and the inner singing—

the ideals look so pretty
all dressed up in their white bows, their sunday school clothes—
but they are not what they seem—then life, of course, is nothing
like what it seems—we are in a state
of perpetual bewilderment—and we are holding the two things
—the ideals and the actual—swaying—
one is like some incredibly tall and unsteady
building you have to crane your neck to see up the side of—
so you feel alternately nauseous and exhilarated—
and the other is like some ocean, endless and dark,
and we are stumbling around on the ocean floor,
kicking up sanddollars, and bumping into coral and whales,
while we think we should be swimming, but in fact
we are those selfsame ragged claws

which is not to say
the position we find ourselves in is so bad—
though it's different from the view we thought we'd have
from the top of that skyscraper—depending
on how you position yourself—but my point is
you don't get to position yourself—

because the positioning happens
of its own accord—*for* you, as it were—
so what we are doing is more like a
continual *re*-positioning in relation to
something—we don't know what—that is continually
moving the pieces, changing the scene

      and the result—well, there is no end result—
is some elaboration—not quite intended—
with a kind of allure, and a kind of
disappointment—with something sort of funny
and something terribly sad—and something
that is a great relief—this elaboration—
look at it closely—swaying—blue—isn't it,
more or less,
           poetry?

One Kiss

I feel a sharp pain where language limits me. I come to the end
    of its jeweled brilliance. The saying stops.
Yet living continues—far beyond the bright flicker of words.
    All the uncontained like a vast lake, reflective and blue, laughing
at these inky marks, pale shadows,
    the sounds our mouths would make.

No matter how we carve the letters, one kiss
    undoes them all.
Sensations explode through the nerve canals, the brain's
    urgent semaphores signal meanings housed so deep
in the body's library of memories
    we'll never know why
we're ready to pledge our lives
    just to dive once more into the reckless
incandescent darkness of this touch.

Except a kiss holds
    what our speech cannot, a taste
of the unbounded, the sun coming up
    inside the flower—
we'll never grasp it,
    the exact shade and shimmer
of new light after a storm, like the wetness
    and newness after making love.

Or we'll touch and touch again
    like an obsessive lover fingering the locks
that open to a world of fire and sharp song, an annihilation
    we crave yet never quite find
in the rigid troops marching across the page,
    no matter how
our tongues refigure the twenty-six permutations of the alphabet
    into a flux, a wreckage,
a monument to the changeless.

We crush them, the letters,
    for the sweet juice, running red and purple
through our fingers, staining us indelibly,
    the river in our veins.

Opening

Sunlight
         falls, spreads shadows
across the blown-out porch,
         green paint peels to rotten wood,
black cat skulks across the yard
         —*swish, swish*—

and all the little stones lie about
         soaking up earth-damp and sky-damp,
a quiet population in the dust.

We undertake our lives, their steady
         hum and riddle, sleepwalkers stumbling
after a defter incantation, blood
         under our blood, traffic on the celestial highway.

If I am writing to come into this,
         you, dear reader, are helping me,
reflecting through the blind spots,
         patient, silvery mirror.

Sun behind a cloud, then out again,
         brighter than ever.

Crickets devouring
         the trees—*clack clack* and *whir*—
squirrels up to no good, sweet chirp
         of birds among the camellias, cheep cheep
of one that sounds
         like a plastic toy. Everything shifts:

The apple tree pulling out of bloom
         into fruit, the light,
how it modulates the apple tree, the grass

now tall and green, rose bush on the verge
of budding, shadow's slant
        and intensity, even my hungers,
off and on like light.

Yet some things are steady, renewing:
        you know or can guess what they are.
Some things hold
        as if caught in a web
like these leaf bits and seed pods floating
        under the porch steps in air.

I come back
        to the routine and the regimen, the implacable hungers
of the flesh, its coat of sadness,
        the spirit revolving within, revving its engines,
ready to fly up, to shout.

Clouds cover the western part of the sky,
        sun in the east, unshadowed,
flies in a mating dance.
        Still we have this:

how the red leaf dangles,
        spins by an invisible thread,
how what's true
        steps outside of every rule,
how what happens next
        we don't know.

Chiaroscuro

There is a kind of darkness
    despite the sunlight
pouring over everything—
    the white pickets of the railing lit,
little saints so rigid and upright—
    despite the warmth its rays give off,
the wasps trying to burrow through the wall
    to get to the other side.

What is this eagerness for otherness,
    for anywhere else to go?

The apple tree is crazed with blossoms.
    Even in a hailstorm
she seems to shout for joy
    the earth littered with her white petals,
trying to take back the red car
    parked underneath,
trying to claim it as one of her own,
    and almost succeeding.

Scriabin vs. the Birds

The day's a lit branch,
    held out, arm's length, glittering,
inviting us to take it,
    take it in. Silence
filled with muted calls of birds,
    Scriabin filtering through the walls.

So quiet the calls of birds are a delicate *pianissimo*,
    interrupted by the cacophony
of a distant rooster crowing.
    The world so still
there's nothing to add to it.

So I watch and listen,
    when so much saying seems a waste,
when even Scriabin, perfectly tuned
    to this morning mood, sounds like indoor art,
something he was doing when he might better
    be out in this.

Perhaps where he was,
    was grey, a rainy city, little to see
but pavement and grime,
    the hustle bustle.

I give thanks for his creation
    even as it falls short
of this light caressing my skin,
    putting coins of silver in the trees,
falls short of the filigree of this subtler score,
    so exquisite in its detail, so fine.

Hymn

The squirrels today on the rooftops,
are wild with advancing spring,
come to the end of their stashes,
tired of the small caves of old trees,
they stick their heads up like the crocuses,
confounded by nature's repetitions.

And I too am lost and wild,
bewildered by this profusion,
racing my rough tongue
over the riverbed of syllables,
chanting this one hymn.

No One Turned Away for Lack of Funds

for Mary Oliver

Everyone has their teachers,
I think to myself this morning
as I notice you have dedicated
your small great book of poems to James Wright.

We are all in each other's debt,
all filled with these inconstant echoes—
inherited vocables, lost syllables—
speaking themselves again in our mouths.

The squirrel is gnawing at the inside
of the kitchen walls. All day I hear her slow,
determined ratcheting. She will find her way
through to something.

I turn back to your poem.
Watching is what you do
so well. Watching until
the words come.

And you are slow and timely
and do not hurry over the least thing
until every leaf is
upturned toward the light.

Look how abundantly
the earth scatters her gifts—
pine needles litter the red ground—
such surplus, such redundance,

as if she were crowing, *plenty, plenty, plenty,*
while we shadow and cringe,
grousing *never enough,*
foolish in our small, square lives.

Now here I am to ply my hand
wherever my own secret lies,
in some hoard, like the acorns
piled swiftly behind these

yellow walls—
my stash, my sweet supply.

Sonata

Feast your ears
 on the rhythmic drumming
of the woodpecker, one little bird
 snickering like a mischievous boy.

This is the balm of morning,
 everything in cahoots:
dark purple
 petunias shuddering
to the same pulse
 as the clack of insects,
a shrill cheep
 from the canyon below
piercing at
 precise intervals,

and when the leaf lets go
 the branch, when the neighbor
sings out to his dog, the way
 someone's radio drones
a low undertone, or a cloud drifts
 a high soprano
over the whole arrangement,
 even the ponderously slow
bass carillon of new growing
 trees thrums the continuo
of this harmony; nothing mars
 the perfection
of the score, nothing
 darkens the day.

II

Adagio mesto

Small Rooms

The day is a damp fire dying down.
I am enclosed in my small rooms:

      memory, discord, desire.

I've walked these halls so many times—
poetry hung like tapestries to light my way
with gold and crimson threads, with bright and dark
      threads, with blood and riches.

I am crying into a small cup
as if it were important
      to save these tears.

I am so tired I no longer know my own name.
I am so empty I am a black book,
      pages of soot, on which you might scrawl your signature
      as on a chalkboard,
stark relief.

Except the thought of you scrawling on me now
feels like sharp blades etching my skin. I am grass
      pressed down into the soaked face of the earth,
      made to lie down, to lay low.

Overhead the sky ridicules with its cold blue.
Way back in distant memory someone loved me once.
      I never should have turned that love away.

Look at me now, empty-handed, with broken
      teeth. Look at me.

Mesto for Solo Violin

for my teacher Lou Calabro, 1926-1991

I am waiting for the song to end,
　　　the dark song, the one
flowing through these bones.

But who is waiting?
And who is singing?

Who is this I
　　　I write from? These cells
once filled with radiance,
　　　now a laden weight.

The sadness descends
　　　its stairsteps *arpeggio*,
traces curves around
　　　the tibia and ulna,
the bones that hold me
　　　in this shape known as I,
diminuendo but more or less
　　　the same, this form—
sonata, partita, fantasia—
　　　that shifts even as it congeals.

Mesto was the word Lou loved
　　　to inscribe on his compositions—
mesto meaning mournful, sad.

If I could savor this inner concerto
　　　in all its movements—
agitato, doloroso, allegro molto—
　　　to listen in the rapture
so easy when I hear a string quartet
　　　bowing *largo maestoso*

a grave lament or a trio
     of winds *vivace*—

If I could tune the same ear to my blood—

Only This

I wanted to burn you, but tender. Not even
my words can do that now. I have no idea

how poetry works, only I know
I don't want to make you suffer.

It's not in the doing: Like lovemaking,
it's something else that happens underneath.

I watch the thin red slant of a girl's mouth,
her carefully defined eyelashes. In me there is no art.

There aren't going to be any of the beautiful
words—strident, luminescent, whatever-the-fuck.

There isn't going to be anything
take-your-breath-away. Only this

terrible emptying. My body
still carved with light

two days after you last made love to me.

Saint Martin in the Fields

this morning my body wrapped like a cord
the little stone in my chest knocking in its cavity
though the sun strikes rose-gold

on the evergreens and a man on the radio
speaks of the academy
of saint martin in the fields and i think how

all our academies
ought to be in the fields where we might
consider the lilies and learn—

now another man speaks of "last night's massacre"
as if it were a nightly occurrence then the savage beauty
of the orchestra comes on the luring cry

of an oboe and i am lost—the little stone grinds down
there is something i cannot recover from
something like knowledge or blindness

like wandering while the world
keeps flowing past my door
it holds me in its teeth like a riddle

write me tell me the answer

Cadence

for Paul Celan

the silence of the silenced

blown-over
snow-tracks

i hear and i
sing back
with my own
damaged tongue

their voices'
falling cadence

that light

i am here
at the far end of the century
that buried you

in drifts

here at the end
of the message-in-a-bottle
that worried you and held

i feel your snow-comfort
your ice-
comfort
whatever comfort
blisters now

radiant, echoic

Bridge

What is it we are after
on this bridge, in the frozen
solitudes? What simple
act of kindness will bind us
forever? What is it
might solve us, absolve us? What brilliant
glimmering now gone?

How shall we survive
the tempest that swirls
around our thin boat?
How are we to live
in such a gale
of grief and becoming?

Where is the rock, that stalwart
homecoming we could cling to? Where
is the break
between the clouds?
Where is anything
wholly good
that doesn't evaporate
or wind up
forgotten among a pile
of weeds and bills?

We ache with the same ache.
We burn, dimly, with the same
knowing. We are alive
with the same turbulent
blood. Dreams
swim in our eyes. Our hands
reach for the same touch.

Hinge

i take a single word, make it play out, splay out, magnified. almost any word will do. almost. *which door leads to heaven?* i once asked, and got the surprising reply, *any*. now it seems i can't find any door and am left in the dark holding shadows. i don't know my own name, so you will have to whisper it for me. here, in my ear. there is no remedy for this, for love.

•

if any poem will do, which one hinges on a world worth waiting for? which one opens like legs, inviting you in to the mystery, wet and huge? does a poem ever open this way, contain this much pleasure, gratitude, passion, pain? can it ever make us cry out in the original tongue? i will lick the salt from your body.

•

you have given me a river in which to drown myself or learn to swim the rapids. should i thank you for this? you have stolen my tongue. my darkness hinges around something deeper and more true, something i fear you run from, something i might not know the way back from. i am willing to go there anyway.

•

now my hands break open like flowers, cresting the earth, soil bed of our shame and shadow, these pasts and bad habits we carry like laundry baskets on our heads, soaked and heavy, mired in this. i would shuck them to come into you, which is coming into myself. i risk the translation.

•

this is going to be a long story so i am afraid to begin it, afraid my words will erode you, though i want to wash you like the sea, want you to wear at me again and again. i am carrying my fingers like blossoms to the gateway of your skin. together with me make one, pressed flat, fanning out, inevitably joined in this butterfly dance. chrysalis. becoming. this is my invitation.

Becoming Pearl

to love is pearl medicine
terrifying transformation
oozing grit and spit
unwinding to original aura

to love is to give up the ideal
find orchids in the muck
overcast freckled paradise
a ladder a painful door

you give me granite and agate
hard shine an eden where people eat
sleep fuck cry laugh
where we sharpen our pencils

to praise the ordinary
i resist it all
wanting effulgence
you give me the thick tang of reality

a cup filled with my own history
and evasions
i'm rattling the bars of the cage
drink up you say drink up

Valley

I have learned to walk in the valley of my fears
    and losses, my thin griefs drawn tight
like shrouds. I have learned to keep moving,
    to keep my tongue light and the roads of my want
stretched before me like ice you might break through.

We get no guarantees. That is what shatters us.
    I would trade this longing
for that one—my home-bound homelessness
    for a wanderer's heart, my dream of heaven
for another night with you.

But God isn't taking any bargains
    this sun-struck afternoon.
I listen to the river of wind, hold up my chapped hands,
    spilling over with green light of a new spring,
still answerless in the hollows of my heart.

Gathering Fall

The crepe myrtle's bright magenta stands
on the eastern rim, hiding behind tall evergreens,
pocked with small ornaments. My life
has slipped away, thirty years folded
like a leaf. Still I hope to flame out
against a green and ochre field—
cherry, Japanese maple, holly, birds,
burnt grass scorched by summer sun.
Now mornings turn cool, sun rises lower.
My life flits in the green, barbed leaves,
hopelessness come as sudden as the morning's chill.

The Grieving and the Dying

The grieving and the dying
just go on and on. It's amazing
what a life they have,
this life of loss.

How is it the birds
singing and chirping this morning
are so unconcerned by this,
do not even know

loss's name? How could we humans
think we are better
than the animals, a life of suffering
superior to a life of song?

You'd do me a great kindness,
you gods, to let me come back
with flight and music as my only goals.
They are my only real aim now,

but I don't reach them
with the ease the birds do—
and then there's love,
the hook where I am caught

and the flesh
around my mouth tears,
and I bite down harder,
unwilling to let go.

Autumn Blues

Autumn has put on its brittle shell,
or taken off. Half-naked and too skinny
in a rust-colored negligee, the oaks striptease
to the high ice-music
of the shifting pallor of the sky.

The photograph captures
an instant, story
captures a thread. Nothing's
gospel, just a little reflected
radiance, motes adrift
in a shaft of sun.

That's what
our lives are. We're not
after unvarnished truth.
Truth, yes, but varnish
is what we're all about,
the glossy veneer, protective coat.

Sun in hiding now,
the Sierra dreaming of snow.
So far there's just this
gold and copper lingerie
strewn on the forest floor,
scattered on the green altar
of the outstretched arms of cedar,
a counterfeit clothing for these evergreens.

What is revealed
in this paring down? What gets unhoused
in me as autumn's candle sputters?
Some small ache burrows,

a mole in the dark, seeking comfort,
isolation, as the temperature
drops and the holidays
begin their unstoppable
procession.

      Movies, books, a nap on the couch,
anything will do
to elude this feral
feeling. Winds of the season,
nothing more.

California Fall

Late October. In the garden, crocuses
push up through the leaf fall.
Everything's confused here. It's California,
caught in weird, autumnal thrall.

Like a page thumbed open to weathers,
wrinkled and rain-soaked,
California's flighty liturgy of the unreal
tips westward into the sea.

Here in the low Sierra, camellias mingle
with the flash and flame of migrant maples,
old emblems planted by homesick pioneers,
hungry for a different gold.

What is it we gather to ourselves,
wanting to bloom even as the dying
begins, as the season yearns for completion?
What is it unravels as the new ravelling starts?

There's no summation in California.
We tremble at the tip, but never fall.
We linger too long and lose our scope,
and drift into the endless sea, headlong into the West.

January Blues

People are clinging to the rafters for a thread
or shred of music—the banging
against our bodies of anything bigger
than we are. Rain sluices
the café windows—cold and fucking wet—
but a thin man plays the fiddle and our bones
shudder for the life the dead cat sings.

Everyone everywhere has lost their mind.
So how do we continue,
post-apocalypse, as it were? I'm not willing
to be polite. Even the baristas
are pounding the cups in time.

Carry me away with your blues then.
The rain's not letting up anytime soon.

The More You Break It

". . . the more you break it,/the nearer it comes to whole." —*Mark Doty*

Is it true—what shatters us
day after vanishing day
is how we are being annealed
into the fullness
that we are?

Our salt tears, like pieces of glass
meant to catch the light,
capture it, reflect some truth
hidden in us
we were blind to in our happiness.

When the light was not
fractured, when we didn't know
we needed the very force—
destroyer, ruthless—
how it goes in a circle.

And we can only approach
when every fragment is fragmented—
hammered, splintered, strewn, spent—
when it lies glittering,
white sand on a beach.

Not to make a prayer
of suffering but to find solace
in the knowing
that this destruction,
these shards of the mirror—

we can only come nearer
when we come through
the fire, burnished, reflective, so that we see,
ourselves, as we are,
in this broken mirror, whole.

Peaches

this morning i looked
into the gleaming
white plastic compost bucket—
three rotting peaches turned blue all over—
and thought of you
and all that's rotting,
all that gives fruit, lets fruit fall,
perishes, all that was once
golden, perfected,
offered itself freely
in the painted enamel bowl
until a blueness began to crawl,
hidden at first,
from the underbelly on up,
embracing, covering,
becoming peach, peach-mold, blue
peach, too tender, flesh falling,
so it's cast on the heap
where the fallen things, the rotten things,
what's spent or no longer needed,
the inedible portions,
wait in the placid harmony of the useless
to become new life again

Another Dose of Pleasure

for Mark Doty

1
Ravaged by grief and loss, by losing,
he nursed his lover through the diminishing

hours, watching and recording
as once-cherished faculties, loved pastimes

were stripped away, and life revealed
itself to be:

perilous, inconstant, perplexing, unspeakably
beautiful;

as friends and acquaintances fell
in startling numbers in the same

unstoppable plummet
toward death or bereavement—

those were the choices then—he wrote, refusing
to be silenced, as the sea

corroded the dunes, and the dunes, in answer, broke
out in resplendent bloom,

as storms trashed the harbor, the seaside town,
then left it glittering, somehow

more radiant in the morning light.
"Tell me where they end,"

he wrote, observing how
fog blurs the line between land

and sea, sea and sky, observing
how the edge of death

is made hazy by love.

And when it had all been taken,
burned, hollowed out, and he woke

and saw the sea still shimmering, the sky
an unrepentant blue, he asked for just one thing:

more.

2

This is our life. We take it on and wear it,
ragged kimono of glimmering threads,
trustworthy sheath and companion.

Our own peculiarities
as familiar and warm to us as bread,
as smooth stones rubbed long between our hard hands.

We learn by doing.
This is the inescapable rhythm,
bitter tang of truth.

How could we do otherwise
but take what's given, swallow it whole,
greedy for more, another dose of pain please,

another dose of pleasure.

III
Allegro grazioso

Angel of Mercy

The birds have fallen silent with the night.
Now the heart calls with her rich music
of dissent and longing, uproar and forgiveness,
hearkening to the world.

You despair over your own imprisoned
soul, while the heart sings high
in a great tree, so high at times
you cannot hear the singing.

You despair over time
for wonder and creation
while wonder and creation unfold
like sheets unfurling in a bright wind.

Do not despair.
Each moment a poem unwinds from seed.
Render sunlight that renews the day.
Render birdsong that calls the dawn.

Reveal your wounds to the sun
by watching
clouds on the wing
dissolve into the grandness of air.

These ten toes are all you have
to grip the ground, your fingernails
turning to new moons. No need
of edits and revisions, recriminations and regrets.

Look, the stars are beginning
to pop out of the black backdrop
of heaven. Look, the timeless
is twirling the hands of the clocks again.

Reach into that blackness
and find you are home there.
Find a velvet darkness to enfold you,
a love you never have to earn.

You tried so long, you did so much.
You asked and sought. Now,
put down your wandering pen,
put down your aching sorrow.

Touch the gladness
at the base of all being,
within every
stone and sigh.

Touch the gladness
in your own
rich song, the soulful earth
that calls to you: Touch.

Wild Earth

Wild earth, wild sky,
how many times
have the stars sung
my name,
and I failed to listen?

How many years
have the trees
been longing
for my embrace
while I stood apart?

How long has the earth
risen to meet me
and all things
conspired to bring forth
my true unfolding

while I stumbled
into walls
muttering
alone, alone, alone

worn thin,
guarding against
the worst, all the while
the earth calling
for my touch?

Since the day of my birth
the river has been flowing,
ready to carry me
while I paddled furiously
mustering my will.

Now my heart breaks
open, hearing the singing,
leaning my face
against the cool of a rock
that reaches for me.

The structures that held
my life, the false edifices
of fear, obligation,
guilt give way

and I stand
in wonder, humbled
not knowing
who I am.

The Heart

Impossible organ,
beating and pumping our blood river
to some unknown sea.

It doesn't take much, a small glitch
weatherbreak, wind-howl
and we are set adrift.

We long for order,
but the heart
with its incessant

thump-thump   thump-thump
has its own music, its own reasons,
if you can call them that.

Today the sun rises gold as it always does,
washes the buildings across the way
with autumnal light, and as the squalling of birds

mingles with the morning traffic,
the heart wakes too
into its colors and weathers,

the way the wind
animates the leaves outside the window,
the way red catches the eye.

Where Everything Is Music

"We have fallen into the place where everything is music." —*Rumi*

How often the heart shatters,
as if shattering were its purpose.
Shards rain as a loved one

leaves, as a new
revelation tears me open,
as I mourn the self I failed.

Who knew wider had no
limit? Who knew rawness
is the heart's condition?—all this

pouring light would bring
such fullness I nearly
choke on love.

I am swimming and drowning at once,
head barely above water,
then not above. Life

nearly wiping me out. Yet here
in these waves I believe
I can hear

fragments of luminous song.

So I Said

if i can't be with you
i will be everywhere

i go out to the hundred
open bodies of the roses
pressed hunger in the faces
sun's tattered brilliance
to the clamor of the streets
                              unafraid

amazed, permeable, wounded

i go out among the leaves of the day
                              breathing

i will become a part of everything
i will come to where you are

Mirage

meanwhile birds wheel in the moonlight
a fly buzzes on the table
a neighbors strums an old guitar

i'm trying to get to the root of this burning
to come up with some gem
not be left clenching dust

but it's all shifting shadows
did i promise what i can't deliver
or is promise itself a mirage

a haze we rely on
to buffer the illusion of permanence
in a world of shift transformation glaze

i'm watching the gods undo the webbing
i've spun around my heart
watching with concerned fascination

nothing i can do to stop it
neither the spinning nor the undoing
these questions don't matter

look
the moonlight catches the slant of clapboards
fence post wind gust flash of white wings

No King

two finches hover at the feeder like last leaves
last of the hysteria of finches
crowding the feeder for weeks

splashing in the birdbath
hiding in the white roses
that trail the old wooden fence

two hummingbirds chase each other
dazzling flashes of iridescent green and ruby
two goldfish drift in the fountain

one bluejay drinks at the rim
a brown rat pokes his eager face
through a hole in the garden fence

the grey cat watches keenly
these goings-on of the animal kingdom
only it's not a kingdom

complex hierarchies a finely-knit web
but no singular king nor congress
though all are subject

to the same immutable laws
no jockeying for power just
small territorial skirmishes lusts

no dreams of mass conquest unseemly
hoarding though the squirrels
pile acorns in stashes

the wind moving the trees is calmer still
without war entirely
objection or regret

bright leaves wave the wind chime resounds
long branches of the mulberry sway up and down
nearly kissing the ground

Making It Enough

Clatter of insects, whir
of a little bird, urgency

of the body, its unending
thirst for pleasure, tastes

luscious on the tongue, textures
that flatter the hand, rich

aromas, lush harmonies,
melodies that clutch

your heart, dissonance
that grips you to the edge

you teeter on just before
orgasm, electric

guitars' scream and throb,
all this coming

into being and dying, all this
ecstasy and hurry and regret,

all this need and questing and
questioning, all this

love burnishing everything.
It is enough.

The love of beauty, the love
of love, words that melt and ooze

when rolled in the cavity
of the mouth, the eye

that lingers over curves, patinas,
luster, glow—it is enough

to praise—
rühmen, das ists—

and praising, to stand
in a state of grace

at one with the teeming world.

The World as Art

This morning dried flowers scattered on the porch.
One yellow dandelion pokes through a hole
in the side of a metal can,
reclaiming the world once again.

The day is cooler but has the warm dry
smell of summer. The wind an audible
exhale in the trees. And me trying
to order it all into lines—

the uncontainable. I never win.
But at times I inch a step closer
to what's true inside of things—the crazy
disarrangement of wild grasses,

a pattern so delicate and right,
it could be a Japanese ink drawing
only better—the continuous
art-making of the world. I bow to it.

White Period

after Cy Twombly

the white dots
                  want to make a space
        where we are nothing
           but silence
nothing
         but thin trails
               through the quiet
less than minor
         unessential
                where we find relief
      in the minutiae
           that don't include us
flecks of yellow
           hints of pink
      but all erased by the white
              and scratched over
         with nothingness

yet these lines
      mean something to our lives
       mean and don't mean us
            reflect a world outside
       mirrored within
                  beyond conscious thought
a place before
      our birth
          where the movement

of silent atoms

drew such lines

that we remember now

Prayer

The poem
is a prayer—
tendril, wind machine,
shimmer, plough—
how we cling

to the words, little
paupers, poor saviors.
It sputters
and burns,
touching us here,

singeing the tips
of our fingers, our
hair—
and yet
what houses us

(most deeply)
is what what we cannot
enclose
what flies out every time.
We are most

set free
by what we can't
catch. And where
I try to reach
and miss, where I

fall short
fall flat
there
You are
most radiant

there You meet
and touch
me
again
and again

burning
my body
to ash,
to holy
ash.

Let Evening Come

after Jane Kenyon

Let evening come with her shadows, all bangles
and sorrow in the silver light. Let evening come
with her grey silks, her blue silks, her soft scents,
her mantle of stars. Let evening come with her handful
of moonlight sprinkled carelessly
on the new-mown grass. Let her shake loose
her long black hair full of lights. And let us shudder
at the beauty and wonder of it, another day.

Let evening come with her pockets full of secrets,
doling them out to her children, that we sleep,
clutching them through the night. Let evening
come, the birds settle in the trees, give up
their ceaseless music, fall silent with the listening
that falls over all things. And let us join hands
with the trees, the stones, with the good
green earth, and sigh, releasing the day, the sins of the day,
its long worries, our straying from the path.

Let evening come like balm, like the gentle lover
who comes in the night. Let her come,
shaking tassles of dew over the land, over the living,
the graves of the past, over the newborn
cradles, the dinner plates unwashed, over the stubble
in the fields and the gravel in the drive,
over the ashtray on the porch, the old man with his lonely
cigarette, its firelight the only warmth left
in his solitary life. Let evening come

and remind him of all he has to praise,
of his past days, his childhood pranks, boyish
yearnings, his flights—the girl

caught behind the shed, the new shoe
lost in the river's pull. Let evening come too
to the old woman with her pot of tea, her quilts
and collections, her rocking and humming,
her songs that come as evening comes,
relentless and full.

Let evening come and we will stand
and give thanks, and not be afraid.
Let it come and we will say
with one voice: Amen.
Let evening, Let it, Let it come.

You Have Permission

to want beauty to press it into the bone
to gather in the storm howling into the wind
to want manna and a heaven to shelter us

to long for the warm tide of arms
to believe in the broken bones mended
to cast in stone and bronze

to know you are separate in the same breath one
how fragile the illusion
of the body is

to dance inside your clothes
you can't help it
we are strung beads on god's necklace

learning a new old language of love
no matter how you stumble
over your feet over forms

there's a deeper freedom
a stronger grace
if you look up in the sky

do it now
birds clouds moon
or inside your own hollow body

you will know
what i mean and come running
into this vast embrace

Wanted

I need the loud girl
that everyone admires
to run over and give me
a hug

in the middle
of all those racing
feet, the mad pursuit
of the ball, no
explanation—

then she's off running
and I am left standing
in the sunlight of the playground

suddenly made radiant, suddenly
wanted
and I go screaming,
tearing after the ball.

What the Flowers Know

Keep climbing, they say, burn
in the blur of the day. Don't lose sight
of the sleight of hand.
That's God up there on stage,
we are puppets in this play. But not
idle puppets and no cruel play, despite
what seems, the seams tearing open, the very fabric
of the world rends, certainly this flesh—but no,
say the bright wilting
petunia heads half-eaten by snail—
no, they say, you cannot
deny the beauty of form,
the peace of the world, the unrelenting
peace—we stand here
and praise the day, the caterpillar
that gnaws through the stalk,
the cat that pisses in the pot—no,
we stand in solid praise
and our word
is as good as God.

Make Me Play

Where am I standing? The ground gives way.
I become you and you
me in the strange alchemy of love. This restlessness
is one form of the Divine in motion. Let it pour out
all over the ground and into the sky.

Boat tossed in a great storm. Who is the self
in danger of splintering? Why so joyful
at the impending wave? Give me
inundation, merger, cells dancing in the spray.
I let my parts fly into the atmosphere.

Who can stop them anyway? I let the gods
sear me with their fierce music.
Do it to me again, I say.
Make me your instrument.
Make me play.

Notes

PENUMBRA—The definition of the word comes from the Merriam-Webster Dictionary and does not include all the definitions given.

THE LANGUAGE OF CLOUDS—was inspired by a beautiful book on clouds I found in a library in Johnson, Vermont. I was struck by the beauty of the language used to describe clouds and the ineffable beauty of the images of the clouds themselves.

THE MORE YOU BREAK IT—The quote by Mark Doty is from his poem "Principalities of June," which appears in his book *Source*.

ANOTHER DOSE OF PLEASURE—was inspired by a Lannan Literary Lecture given by Mark Doty. He read from his poems and memoirs, including wrenching writings about the death of his lover from AIDS. When the interviewer asked him what he wanted in his life now, he answered, "more." I was incredibly taken by the courage and love of life in that answer. The line "Tell me where they end" comes from Doty's poem "Fog Argument," which appears in his book *Atlantis*.

WHERE EVERYTHING IS MUSIC—The quote comes from a poem of the same name by Rumi from *Rumi—Selected Poems*, translated by Coleman Barks and John Moyne.

MAKING IT ENOUGH—The quote is from Rilke's *Sonnets to Orpheus*, part I, number 7. It means, "To praise—that's it!"

PRAYER—The quote is from Hafiz's poem "Troubled," which appears in the book of his poems *The Gift*, translated by Daniel Ladinsky.

LET EVENING COME—was inspired by a poem of the same name by Jane Kenyon, which was read as a prompt at a workshop I took.

WANTED—The quote comes from *The Duino Elegies* by Rainer Maria Rilke, translated by Stephen Mitchell.

Gratitude

I am deeply grateful to the following journals and anthologies for publishing these poems, sometimes in earlier versions:

Borderlands: Texas Poetry Review: "Dark Nets"
Eclipse: "Small Rooms"
Entropy: "No King"
Hardpan: "California Fall"
Inscape: "Peaches" and "Scriabin vs. the Birds"
Jewish Women's Literary Journal: "The World as Art"
Left Curve: "Cadence" (originally title "paul")
Meridian Anthology of Contemporary Poetry: "Sonata"
Nevada County Poetry Series Anthology 2003: "Penumbra"
Nevada County Poetry Series Anthology 2005: "Winter" and "California Fall"
Orbis International Literary Journal: "Gathering Fall"
Poem: "So I Said" and "Shades" and "Prayer"
Rattlesnake Review: "Winter"
Sacred Fire Magazine: "The Heart"
San Diego Poetry Annual: "Bridge"
Slant: "Autumn Blues"
Spillway: "No One Turned Away For Lack of Funds"
Tule Review: "Becoming Pearl" and "The Grieving and the Dying"
Untitled Country Review: "Saint Martin in the Fields"
Westview: "Sonata"

My huge gratitude goes to all the people who have helped this book come into being, my dear friends, family and the exceptional community in which I live.

I wish to thank particularly my music mentor, Lou Calabro, for believing in me and helping me to be an artist; Ed Smallfield, who opened the doors to growing as a poet so many years ago; Parkman Howe, even farther back in time, who introduced me to reading many great contemporary poets; Annie Finch, whose vision, skill and encouragement helped shape this book; David Rigsbee, whose editorial advice, guidance and kindness have been a beacon of light; Rusty Morrison and the Colrain Conference for valuable insight, learning and hope; Molly Fisk, for deep friendship, poetic and otherwise; Indigo Moor, whose extraordinary generosity of spirit helped me cross the finish line; and Finishing Line Press for believing in and midwifing this book. And most especially to my beloved, Don Williams, for his steadfast support and love and his willingness to dive into the adventure of this book with me.

I thank my parents for their love and care and for enriching my life with the arts and with deep thought. And all the poets and writers with whom I have shared workshops and writing groups, including my wonderful students, who teach me so much. Thanks particularly to William O'Daly for the vital spark that got me to hire editors to help with the book. Thanks also to those who gave generously to my GoFundMe campaign to give me the needed funds to hire an editor.

Deep thanks to my patrons on Patreon, whose companionship and support on the journey sustains me in so many ways: Adam Frey, Andi Tilmann, Barbara Raymond, Catharine Wells, Christina Sinatra, Collette LaRocque, Cris Mulvey, Curtis Lauber, Daniel Kennedy, Denise Reynolds, Dina Barzilai, Don Williams, Eileen Hale, Emily Martin, Erika Chin, Harry Brooks, Jack MacKay, Jennifer Putnam, Joanna Robinson, Julie Cobden, Karen Milgate, Karl Snyder, Kathy McKeough, Kristen Strohm, Larren Merriman, Laura Holland Belk, Laurel Wilkinson, Laurie Perla, Lee Auerbach, Liam Ellerby, Lil McGill, Lindsay Dunckel, Lisa Barker, Lynn-Amanda Brown, Marybeth Paul, Matthew Sweigart, Megara Bell, Michael Mauldin, Molly Fisk, Orna Ross, Regina Brunig, Robin Wallace, Ruth Anna Putnam, Sarah Wolf, Susan Rasmussen, Thomas Moseley, Tom Taylor, and Tracy Koppel. It is such a pleasure to share the process of creation with you. I welcome others to join us in this intimate conversation on creativity at Patreon.com/MaximaKahn.

Thank you to the poetry lovers in my town, who have encouraged me for years, and to poetry readers everywhere.

About the Author

Maxima Kahn is a writer of poetry, essays and fiction. Her work has been featured in numerous literary journals and on popular blogs such as TinyBuddha, PositivelyPositive and The Startup. She has twice been nominated for Best of the Net, was a finalist for the *Atlanta Review* poetry contest, and has received scholarships and fellowships to the Community of Writers at Squaw Valley and the Vermont Studio Center. *Fierce Aria* is her first full-length collection of poems.

Having formerly taught creative writing at the University of California, Davis extension, she now teaches and blogs at BrilliantPlayground.com. Her popular workshops on poetry, creative writing and creativity—and her one-on-one creative life coaching—have helped hundreds of people to unleash their creative gifts and create lives of passion, purpose and deep play. She is also an improvisational violinist, an award-winning composer and a dancer.

You can follow and support her creative process and journey at Patreon.com/MaximaKahn. Learn about her workshops and read her blog on creativity and soulful living at BrilliantPlayground.com. And find updates on her writing life, including upcoming events, at MaximaKahn.com.

CPSIA information can be obtained
at www.ICGtesting.com
Printed in the USA
FSHW021847060620
70736FS